Algrove Publishing Limited
36 Mill Street, P.O. Box 1238
Almonte, Ontario, Canada K0A 1A0

Telephone: (613) 256-0350
Fax: (613) 256-0360
Email: sales@algrove.com

Library and Archives Canada Cataloguing in Publication

Lukowitz, Joseph J
        50 popular woodworking projects / Joseph J. Lukowitz.

Reprint. Originally published: Milwaukee : Bruce Pub. Co., 1938.
ISBN-10 1-897030-40-1
ISBN-13 978-1-897030-40-0

        1. Woodwork. I. Title. II. Title: Fifty popular woodworking projects.

TT185.L84 2005   684'.08   C2005-905548-0

Printed in Canada
#2-9-06

PUBLISHER'S NOTE

The author's purpose in this book was to detail projects that could be built using only basic hand tools. Many of the styles are not ones we would make today but the methods of construction and the methods of scaling plans up or down are as relevant as they were 70 years ago, with the exception that nails are specified in many areas where we would use screws today. Screws were used in the trades and in factories in the 1930s but were both expensive and scarce in retail hardware stores.

Leonard G. Lee
Publisher
Almonte, Ontario
December 2005

50 POPULAR WOODWORKING PROJECTS

Jos. J. Lukowitz
Instructor of Industrial Arts
Milwaukee Public Schools
Milwaukee, Wisconsin

1938

Algrove Publishing
Classic Reprint Series

PREFACE

The purpose of this book is to present to teachers a collection of projects that may be used as subject matter for an entire course, or individual projects that may instill variety and renewed interest to present courses. The projects range from the very simple to the quite complex, and therefore, selection may be made for any grade level.

Homecraftsmen, too, will find this book filled with interesting and useful articles to make for the home.

Each project is represented by a clear working drawing, a perspective sketch or photograph, and a short explanatory text where necessary. All unnecessary lines have been omitted so as not to confuse the worker. Suggestions for varying the design and construction are given in a number of instances so that in reality the book contains a number of potential projects besides those described in detail.

All of the projects, except those requiring lathe work, can be constructed with hand tools. This is of special interest to schools and homecraftsmen who do not have machinery but who desire to produce work that is of approved design.

Tables, wall shelves, benches, and stools as well as other small projects are always very popular with students and it is such work that this book features.

Of particular interest is the description and use of patterns or templates which may be used in various ways to aid in the designing and enriching of projects. The use of such patterns will aid the worker to recognize the possibilities of variations in design and will encourage him to be original by offering a number of tangible units as a starting point.

CONTENTS

FIFTY POPULAR WOODWORKING PROJECTS

½" SQUARES

THICKNESS
⅜" OR ½"

⅛"

4½"

¾"

1"

1¾"

WEDGE DETAILS

FASTEN THE CAT TO
THE WEDGE WITH
GLUE AND NAILS

A REGULAR PIECE
OF RIBBON IS TIED
AROUND THE CAT'S
NECK

Fig. 1. A door stop.

DOOR STOPS (pp. 8, 10, 11, 12)

Ever since doors hung on hinges, many methods of holding them either ajar or closed have been used. A stone, a brick, and even a bag of sand were placed to hold it in a desired position. But now the preference is for a decorative door stop. Household pets, especially the cat and dog, are imitated. The construction and painting of these projects affords a pleasant undertaking.

The designs of the door stops in this book are such that it is not absolutely necessary to use plywood in order to avoid splitting. Excellent material for these projects may be obtained from discarded fruit boxes.

When painting the door stops and similar projects, it is best to apply the background or predominating color over the whole piece. After it has dried the contrasting color that brings out the details should be applied.

GARDEN BIRDS (pp. 13, 14)

These birds produce a colorful effect on the lawn and in the garden. It is for this reason that they are in such favor with many craftsmen. A unique feature of the birds in this book is the loop in the wire standard which gives the impression of a bird standing on a limb, when a small branch is slipped through it.

BLOTTER HOLDER (p. 15)

This blotter holder is a decided variation from the rocker type often found. The rocker type is comparatively difficult to construct and for this reason is not included.

BRACKET SHELF (p. 16)

There is always room for a shelf and for this reason one has been included here. In the construction of a shelf many fundamental principles of woodworking are involved making it a good beginner's project.

CANDLESTICK (p. 17)

This candlestick is simple to make and requires only a very little material; scraps may be used which otherwise would be wasted. It will serve as a decorative piece on a mantel or table.

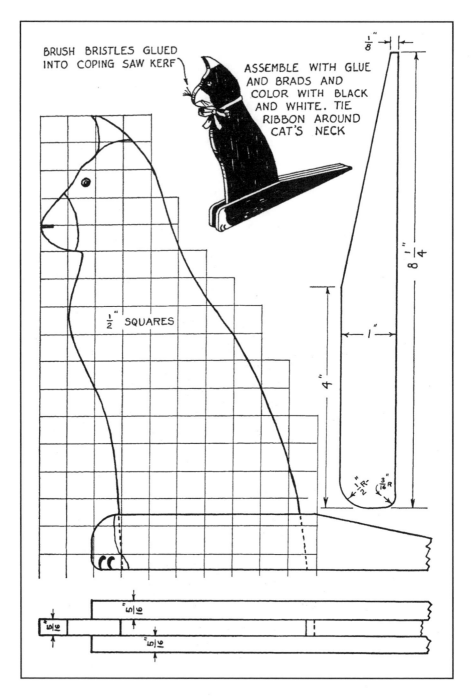

Fig. 2. A door stop.

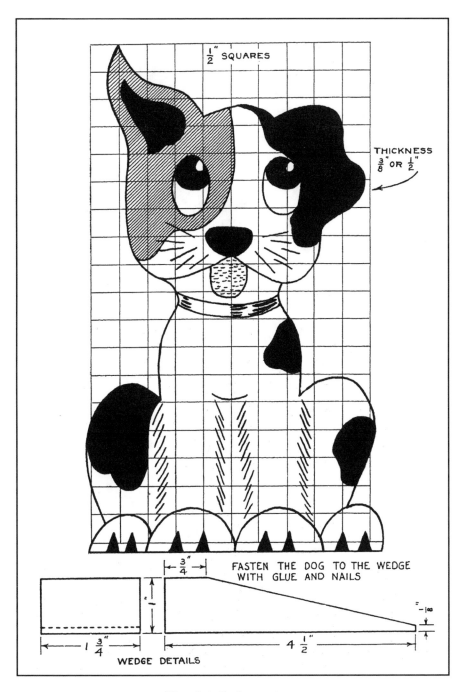

Fig. 3. A door stop.

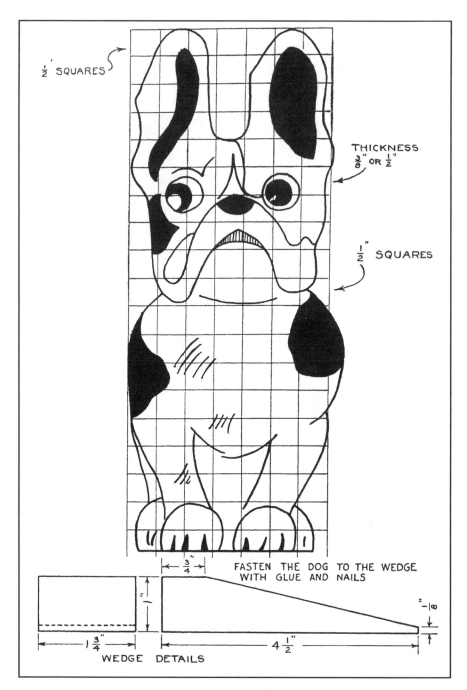

Fig. 4. A door stop.

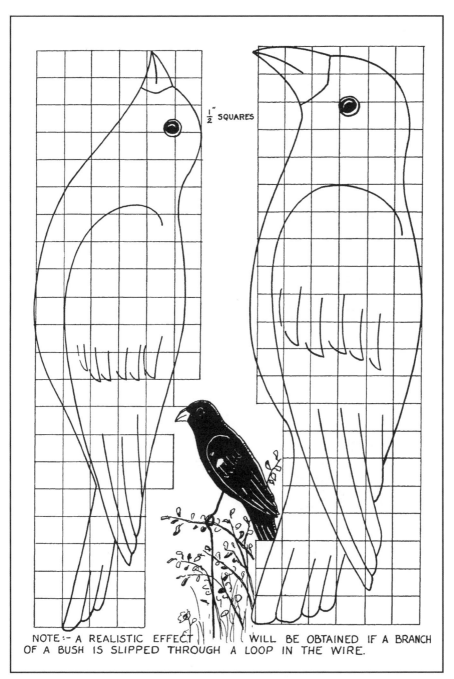

Fig. 5. Garden birds.

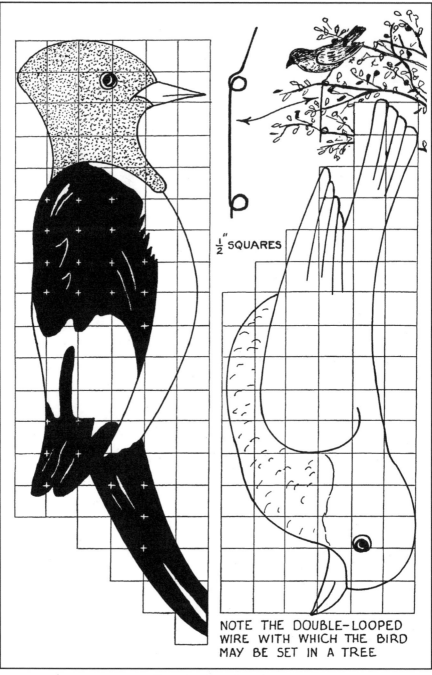

$\frac{1}{2}''$ SQUARES

NOTE THE DOUBLE-LOOPED
WIRE WITH WHICH THE BIRD
MAY BE SET IN A TREE

Fig. 6.   Garden birds.

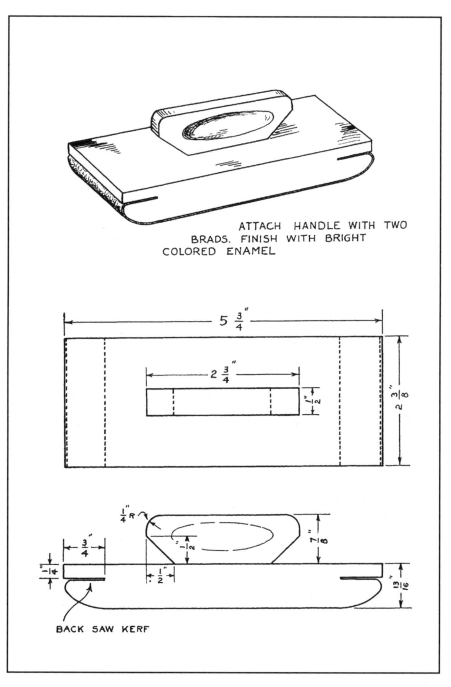

ATTACH HANDLE WITH TWO
BRADS. FINISH WITH BRIGHT
COLORED ENAMEL

BACK SAW KERF

Fig. 7. A blotter holder.

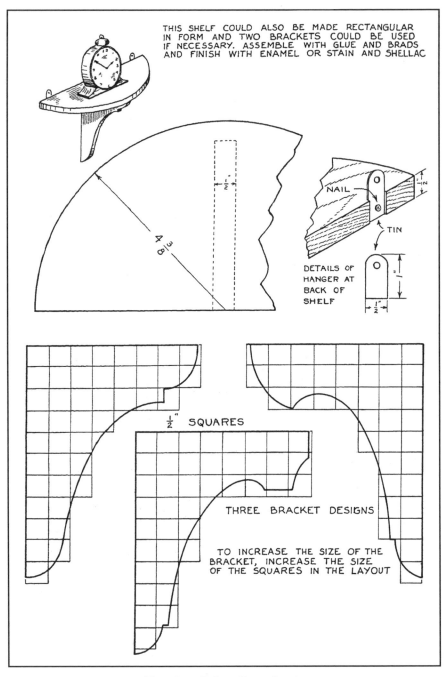

THIS SHELF COULD ALSO BE MADE RECTANGULAR IN FORM AND TWO BRACKETS COULD BE USED IF NECESSARY. ASSEMBLE WITH GLUE AND BRADS AND FINISH WITH ENAMEL OR STAIN AND SHELLAC

$4\frac{3}{8}$

$\frac{1}{2}$

NAIL

TIN

DETAILS OF HANGER AT BACK OF SHELF

$\frac{1}{2}$"

1"

$\frac{1}{2}$" SQUARES

THREE BRACKET DESIGNS

TO INCREASE THE SIZE OF THE BRACKET, INCREASE THE SIZE OF THE SQUARES IN THE LAYOUT

Fig. 8. A bracket shelf.

[16]

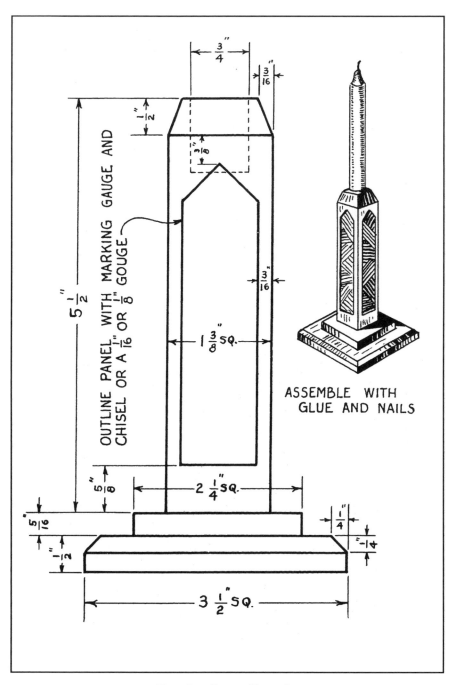

Fig. 9. A candlestick.

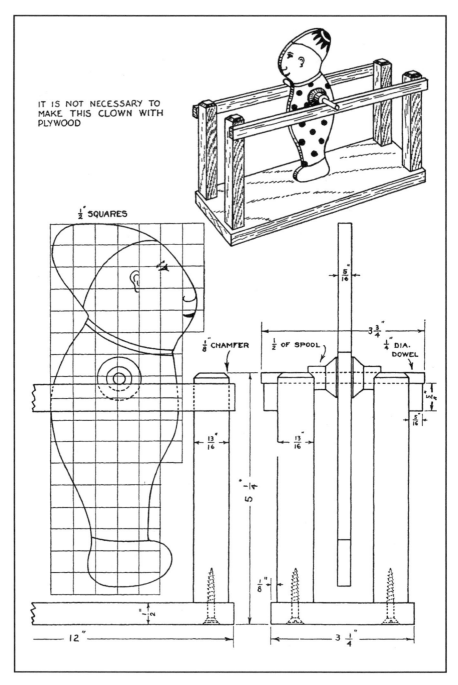

IT IS NOT NECESSARY TO
MAKE THIS CLOWN WITH
PLYWOOD

$\frac{1}{2}$" SQUARES

$\frac{1}{8}$" CHAMFER

$\frac{1}{2}$ OF SPOOL

$\frac{5}{16}$"

$3\frac{3}{4}$"

$\frac{1}{4}$" DIA.
DOWEL

$\frac{5}{16}$"

$\frac{5}{16}$"

$\frac{13}{16}$"

$\frac{13}{16}$"

$5\frac{1}{4}$"

$\frac{1}{8}$"

12"

$3\frac{1}{4}$"

Fig. 10.   A tumbling clown.

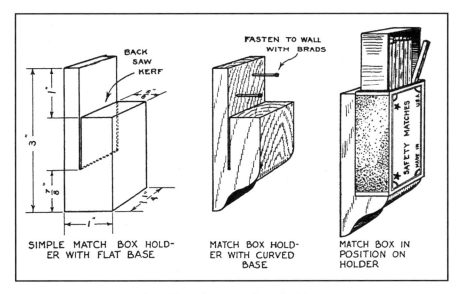

FASTEN TO WALL
WITH BRADS

SAFETY MATCHES

MADE IN U.S.A.

SIMPLE MATCH BOX HOLD-
ER WITH FLAT BASE

MATCH BOX HOLD-
ER WITH CURVED
BASE

MATCH BOX IN
POSITION ON
HOLDER

Fig. 11. A match-box holder.

MATCH-BOX HOLDER

This holder may be constructed easily from a piece of scrap wood and
will keep a box of safety matches ready at hand near the stove or furnace.

TUMBLING CLOWN (p. 18)

This toy clown is a simple variation of the wheel and has been a
favorite project with boys for many years. Its tumbling action will
provide a great deal of amusement.

SMALL GOUGE USED FOR VEINING

A number of projects in this book include in their construction some
more or less optional designs which require veining, that is, outlining
with a small gouge. Figure 12 shows the type of gouge which makes
this work very easy, even for beginners. The small gouge takes the
place of a V-shaped veining tool which is difficult to sharpen and also
difficult to control.

This gouge is known as a straight carving gouge. Either a 1/16- or
a ⅛-in. size will do; the 1/16-in. however, is preferred. Because this
gouge is so easy to handle, it will at the outset instill confidence in the
user and possibly serve as an introduction to relief carving. This type

gouge is not correctly sharpened for this work when it comes from the manufacturer. It will cut well with the grain but in order that it may cut equally as well across the grain, it should be ground away more at the

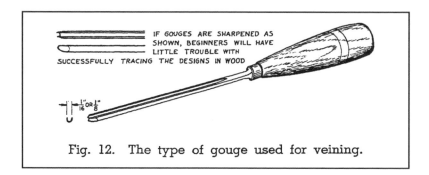

IF GOUGES ARE SHARPENED AS SHOWN, BEGINNERS WILL HAVE LITTLE TROUBLE WITH SUCCESSFULLY TRACING THE DESIGNS IN WOOD

$\frac{1}{16}$" OR $\frac{1}{8}$"

Fig. 12. The type of gouge used for veining.

center than at the sides. These sides of the gouge will score the surface of the wood in advance of the center cutting portion of the gouge.

When in use the gouge is held in both hands, one hand on the handle and the other near the cutting edge. The hand near the cutting edge also rests on the work and controls and guides the gouge.

WALL AND CORNER SHELVES

Figure 13 is an interesting design for a wall shelf especially with pierced or open work in the ends. This shelf has no back at the top or bottom but these pieces may be added (see Fig. 14).

The back at the top and bottom in Figure 14 adds somewhat to the rigidity, but is not absolutely necessary. The scroll and leaf design at the top is shown full size at A, Figure 18. If desired, the scroll alone may be used. The design is outlined in the wood with a 1/16- or $\frac{1}{8}$-in. straight carving gouge (see Fig. 12).

The wall shelf shown in Figure 15, is another open-back construction. The same end design used on this wall shelf is used on the corner shelf in Figure 17, while the corner shelf in Figure 16 has the same end design as the wall shelf in Figure 14.

In the construction of these wall and corner shelves nailed butt joints may be used. The brads should be carefully set and the holes filled. Stop-dado joints may be used for they add much to the rigidity.

Wall and corner shelves are finished with stain, enamel, or lacquer. When enameled, the edges are sometimes set off with a complementary or contrasting color. The edges of stained racks may be decorated in this same manner. Very often hand-painted designs are used.

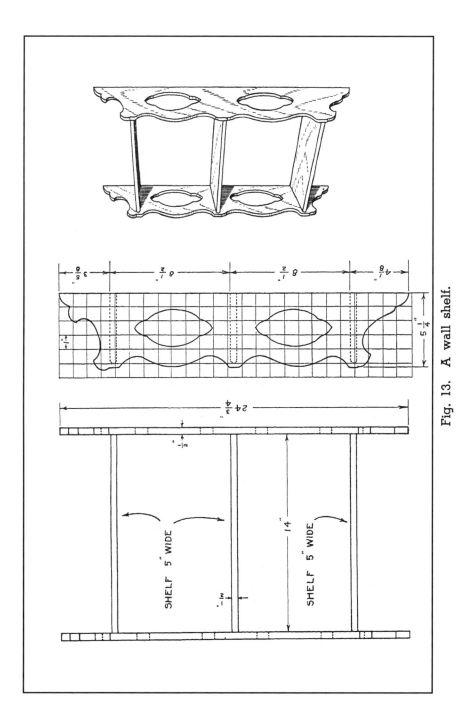

Fig. 13. A wall shelf.

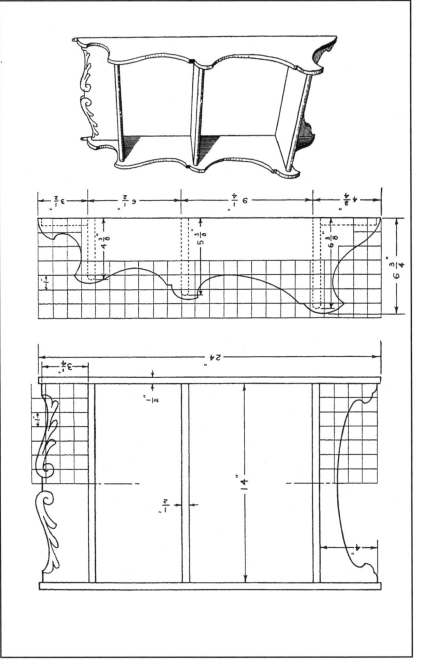

Fig. 14. A wall shelf.

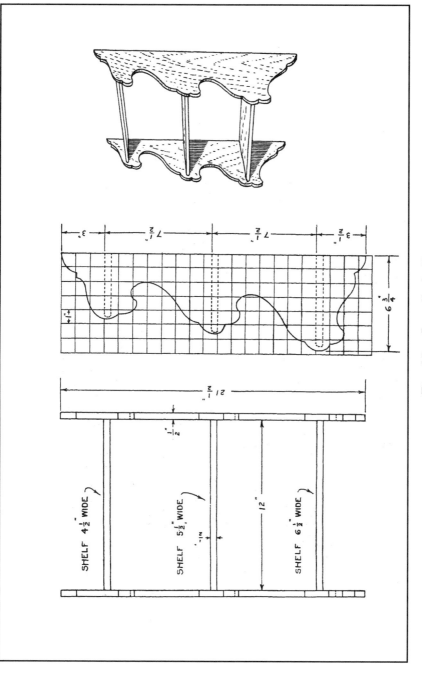

Fig. 15. A wall shelf.

SHELF 4½" WIDE

SHELF 5½" WIDE

SHELF 6½" WIDE

12"

½"

21½"

3"

7½"

7½"

3½"

6¾"

1½"

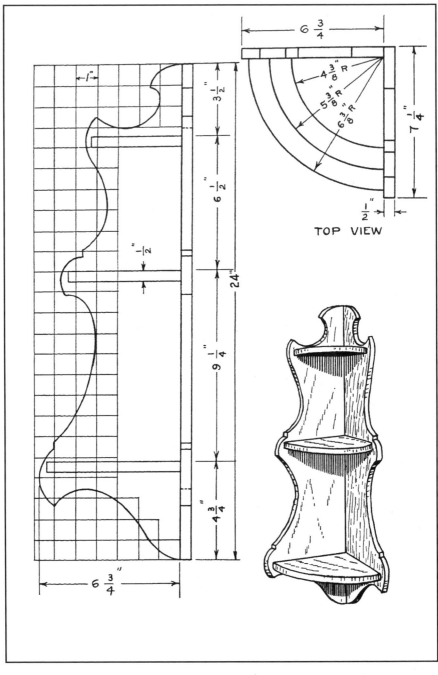

TOP VIEW

Fig. 16. A corner shelf.

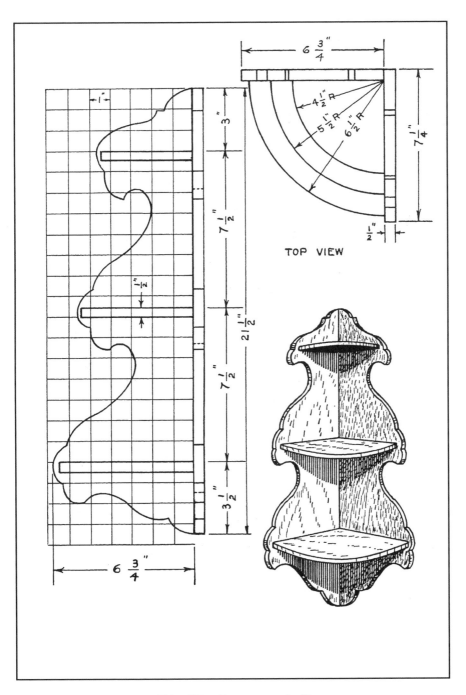

TOP VIEW

Fig. 17. A corner shelf.

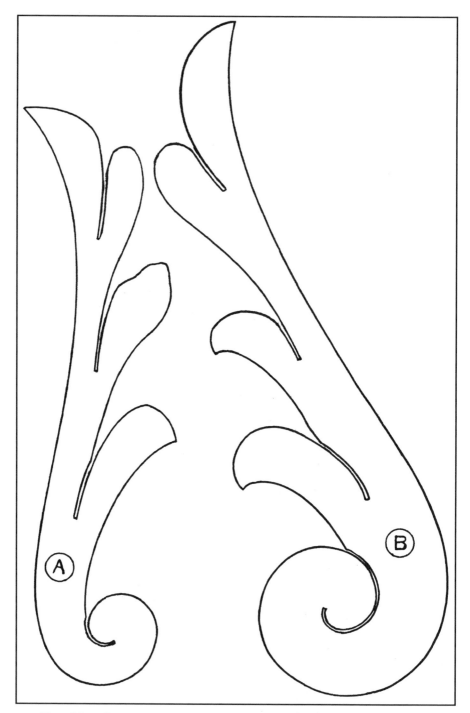

Fig. 18.   Cyma curve and leaf and scroll designs (full size).

METAL TEMPLATES

The leaf and scroll designs in Figure 18 are composed in part of the beautiful cyma curve which is used so much in furniture design. This curve is used frequently alone as contour enrichment and often is combined with a scroll or a leaf and scroll to ornament both contour and surface. Practical applications of these designs are shown in Figures 14, 28, and 49. In each example, one of these templates or patterns (Fig. 18) has been used in whole or in part for the layout of the design. This

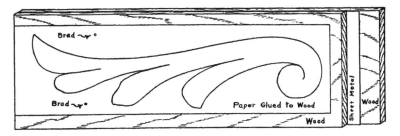

Fig. 19. The method of blocking sheet metal
for cutting with a coping saw.

design has a great many other possible applications. When patterns that allow variation are available in the school shop, boys are encouraged to use some degree of originality in their work.

Templates that are used a great deal should be made of sheet metal. Those made of paper are easily torn, and when used a number of times their edges become quite ragged and they no longer give accurate layouts. Many patterns, because of intricacy of design, cannot be made of wood. In such cases even plywood is not suitable.

Ordinary tin plate or 12-oz. sheet copper is about the right gauge to use for metal templates. Figure 19 shows how the sheet metal is placed between two thin pieces of wood before being cut with a coping saw having a metal-cutting blade. It is surprising how easy it is to control the saw when cutting in this manner. If any filing is necessary after sawing it should be done before separating the wood and the metal.

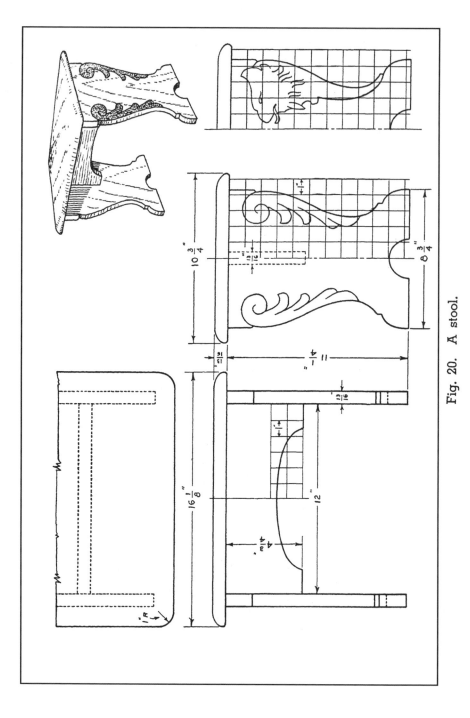

Fig. 20. A stool.

STOOL

The simple stool, shown in Figure 20, is constructed of four pieces of wood and is a popular project with boys of junior-high-school age.

Basswood, pine, or poplar work up very well for this project, and when properly finished with stain, shellac, and wax or varnish, it makes an attractive piece of furniture.

A full-sized pattern for the leaf design which is veined on the ends is shown in B, Figure 18. The text accompanying Figure 18 describes how this and similar patterns may be utilized in various ways as aids in laying out curves and enriching surfaces. If only scrolls are desired on each end of the stool, use the leaf pattern (B, Fig. 18) to trace the scrolls, and leave off the rest of the leaf.

The lion's head at the right in Figure 20, is an alternative design which is very popular with boys, the full-sized details of which are shown in Figure 54.

Assemble the project with roundhead screws, or use flathead screws and conceal the heads with putty.

The leaf designs on the ends first should be water-stained slightly darker than the rest of the stool. Care should be taken not to get any stain in the outside gouge lines. Inside lines, such as the termination of the scroll and the three lines of the leaves which extend inside of the pattern, should be stained. The entire project finally should be stained with either water or oil stain.

If desired, this stool can be upholstered.

Fig. 21. A stool.

WALL PLAQUES

Very popular projects with boys are wall plaques such as shown on page 32. The only tool required for the carving is a small gouge like the one shown in Figure 12. It is very easy to use and control and no difficulty will be encountered in turning out creditable work with it.

In Figure 22 are details of two different shapes for shields. Rectangles,

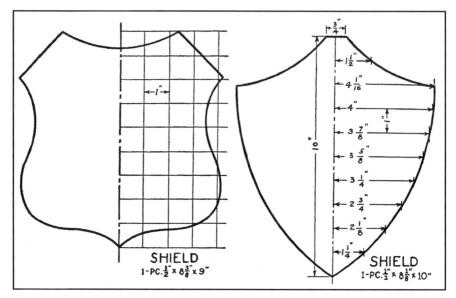

Fig. 22.   Shield designs.

ovals, hexagons, in fact any suitable figure, may be used for this kind of project. Straight-grained pine or basswood are best suited for such carving.

Figures 26 and 27 are full-sized patterns for two popular carving subjects. Because of the wide interest in this work and the great amount of handling which such patterns necessarily receive, it is well to make the patterns of sheet metal as shown in Figure 19.

In Figures 26 and 27 are shown two types of templates. The inside details of the Native American are marked with holes drilled in the template. In the scout template the inside details are sawed. When the latter method is used, tiny pieces of metal are soldered in or over the grooves at various points to strengthen the template.

[30]

Of course, other subjects besides the Native and scout may be used. The daily newspaper sporting page furnishes popular carving subjects in the form of pictures of baseball players, football players, and other representative sports. Such newspaper pictures can be traced onto the wood with carbon paper. Any picture or subject, however, which shows a front view of the human head should be avoided. Such subjects do not

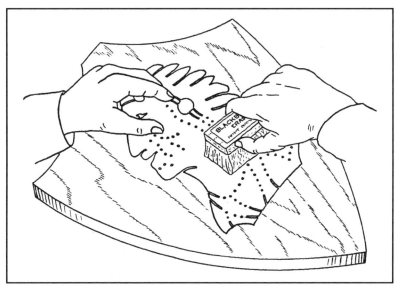

Fig. 23. Transferring the design to the work.

work out well in this type of carving. Subjects having very minute details also should be avoided unless such detail can be eliminated.

When a large group of boys, or an entire class, requires the same template, time can be saved by making a metal pattern or template and then transferring the design to the wood by rubbing over the template with a blackboard eraser charged with any fine, dry color, such as burnt turkey umber or chrome green. A very small quantity of this dry color will make hundreds of reproductions. Practice will teach the amount of powder to be used. The eraser should be rubbed back and forth and crosswise with considerable pressure as shown in Figure 23. The template should be removed carefully and the excess powder blown off. Strange as it may seem, better results are not obtained by tapping the eraser over the template or by using a dry brush with the powder. Figure 24 shows a plaque on which a design has been transferred in the manner just described. The instructor or a boy can transfer a large number of

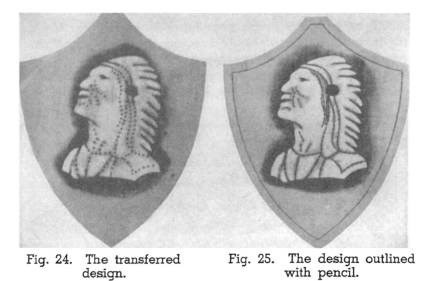

Fig. 24. The transferred
design.

Fig. 25. The design outlined
with pencil.

designs in a very short time by this method. Each boy then should outline the subject and connect the stenciled portions with a pencil. Figure
25 shows the design outlined with pencil ready for carving. A ⅜-in.
border should be scribed with finger and pencil.

It is not necessary to have a gouge for each boy in the class. In a class
of 24, for example, if 12 gouges are available, half of the class may work,

Wall plaques.

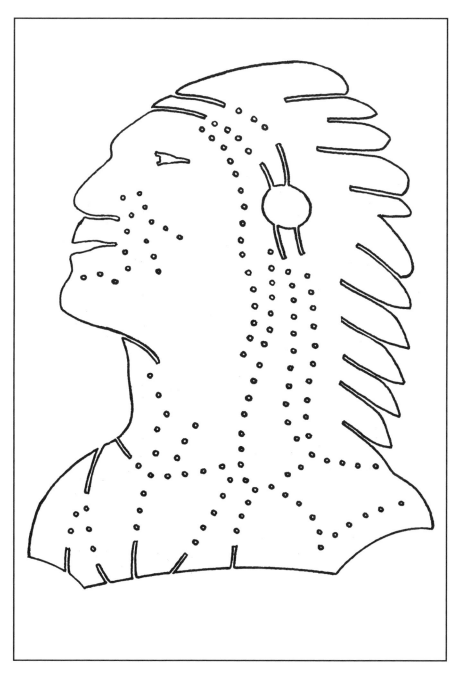

Fig. 26. A Native American (full size).

Fig. 27. A boy scout (full size).

say, ten minutes while the others watch. Then, the other half may work ten minutes. This method will give the boys a chance to rest and better work will be produced.

The plaques on page 32 are finished in the following manner: First, a thin sizing coat of shellac is applied. When thoroughly dry, the plaque is sanded with very fine finishing paper, after which it is thoroughly brushed, especially in the grooves where the dust tends to lodge. Blowing will not remove all the dust. Next, two coats of white enamel are applied, and when the enamel is thoroughly dry, the plaque is antiqued with burnt umber and oil applied with a brush and rubbed out with a rag.

Other finishes may be used. Staining gives a pleasing effect provided the grain markings are not pronounced, thus disturbing the profile. A plaque also may be finished in bright colors and then antiqued.

A door stop. See page 12.

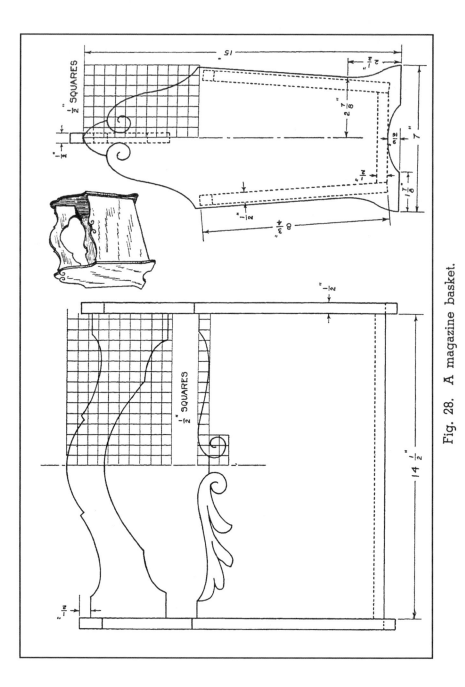

Fig. 28. A magazine basket.

MAGAZINE BASKET

The magazine basket in Figure 28 may be made of pine, poplar, basswood, or any similar wood.

Since this project utilizes only nailed butt joints it will not be too difficult for boys having little ability. Three-eighths-inch material may be used instead of ½-in., but greater care will be required in cutting to prevent splitting, and in nailing to guard against nails coming through the surface.

The design on the sides is shown full size in A, Figure 18. Either the entire leaf or just the scroll may be used to enrich the surface. The leaf may be veined with a 1/16- or ⅛-in. straight carving gouge like the one shown in Figure 12. For contrast, the leaf may be stained a little darker than the rest of the project. The leaf design could also be carved in relief very effectively. If the magazine basket is to be enameled, only the scroll should be used to enrich the surface. The two scrolls on the ends may be laid out with the same pattern (A, Fig. 18).

If desired, the handle may be made much wider to extend well down into the basket to act as a partition. In that case the lower edge of the piece will, of course, be left straight. The use of such a partition will necessitate the cutting of a handhold near the top by which the magazine basket may be conveniently carried. It is somewhat difficult to paint a partitioned magazine basket unless a spray outfit is used.

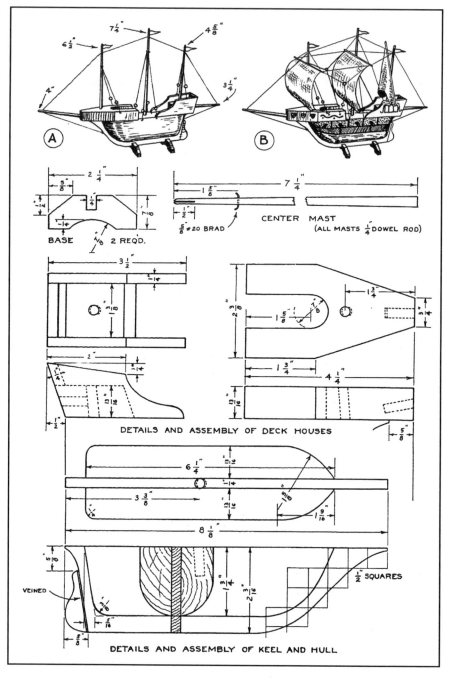

Fig. 29. A ship model.

[38]

SHIP MODEL

Many a boy has looked wistfully at a large, complicated ship model too difficult for him to make. The junior model shown in A, Figure 29, was designed to satisfy the desire that most boys have of wanting to make a ship.

All of the parts entering into the construction of the ship are quite small; therefore, this is a very economical project. It might be possible to utilize left-over pieces from other projects.

The most difficult parts to make are perhaps the two 13/16-in. pieces which make up the hull. After these two pieces are cut to size, they are nailed together. The shaping is then completed. The nails are placed well up toward the top edge, out of the way of the plane, otherwise it may be nicked when shaping the hull. When the hull is completed, including the sanding, the pieces are separated, and the keel is placed between them, and then nailed together permanently.

Tiny screw eyes or staples may be used on the ship as a means of fastening the rigging. Small pieces of dowel may be used as pulleys or blocks in the rigging. An appearance of age may be given to the boat by staining it with a dark brown oil stain. All rigging lines with the exception of the long line connecting all of the masts should be double.

The skeleton rigging shown on the boat (A, Fig. 29) satisfies most boys; however, an elaboration of this same ship with complete sails and rigging, together with decorations and cannons, which are made from dowel rod, is shown at B, Figure 29.

MARBLED PENHOLDERS

Every home and school shop accumulates small pieces of wood which may often be utilized for small objects.

Figures 30 and 31 show several different designs for penholders which may be made from small scraps of material. Figure 30 is a pleasing form of penholder. A, B, and C, Figure 31, show three variations in the design. A and B show a sphere used as a part of a penholder. The sphere may be turned in a lathe. Wooden spheres may be obtained at times from old discarded pieces of furniture, or from spindled archways in old homes which are being remodeled or wrecked. C, Figure 31, represents a double penholder utilizing a cylinder for a part of the design. The cylinder can be turned in a lathe or can be made by hand.

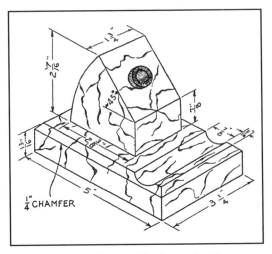

Fig. 30. A marbled penholder.

At B in Figure 31 is shown how the ⅜-in. rubber-socket bushing is screwed into a hole bored into the sphere. The hole should be bored slightly smaller in diameter than the outside diameter of the threaded portion of the bushing. The thread in this hole should be cut by screwing a piece of threaded ⅜-in. pipe into it. The parts of the penholders in Figure 31 should be fastened together with a screw through the bottom of the base. The two parts of the penholder shown in Figure 30, however, should be nailed together.

Before applying the finish to the penholders in Figure 31, the parts should be separated so that the finishing can be more readily done. First, the penholder should be given a thin priming coat of shellac. When thoroughly dry, it should be sanded with finishing paper and given two coats of black enamel. When the second coat of enamel is thoroughly dry, the marbled effect can be obtained as follows: A little daub of cream-colored enamel should be placed on a small piece of scrap wood. Then with a small stick of wood, about the size of a match sharpened to a blunt point (about 1/32 in. diameter) (see D, Fig. 31), the markings

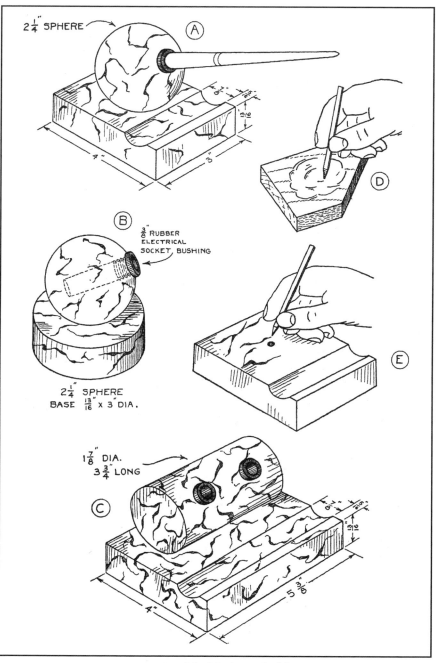

Fig. 31. Marbled penholders.

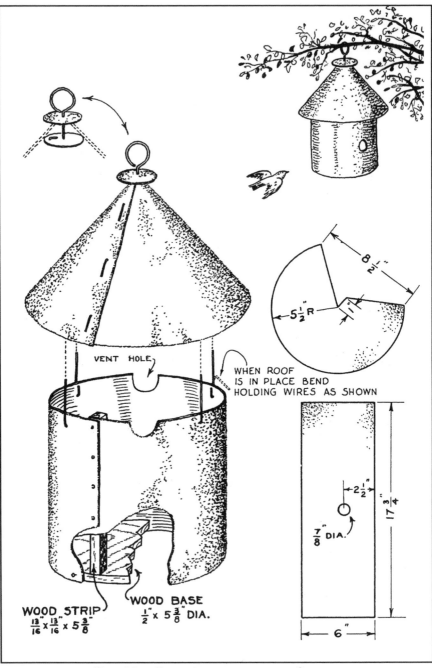

VENT HOLE

WHEN ROOF IS IN PLACE BEND HOLDING WIRES AS SHOWN

$8\frac{1}{2}$"

$5\frac{1}{2}$ R

WOOD STRIP $\frac{13}{16}$" x $\frac{13}{16}$" x $5\frac{3}{8}$"

WOOD BASE $\frac{1}{2}$" x $5\frac{3}{8}$" DIA.

$2\frac{1}{2}$"

$\frac{7}{8}$" DIA.

$17\frac{3}{4}$"

6"

Fig. 32. A roofing-paper wren house.

are made on the penholder as shown in E, Figure 31. A great many different effects can be obtained by using different colors for the streaking or marking. For example, instead of using black for the background, green may be used with a marking of lighter green and a little yellow here and there. White also may be used for a background with markings of gray.

A very small paint brush may be used for the streaking, but a stick is preferred because the width of lines is more easily regulated. The stick makes firm contact with the wood whereas a small brush in the hands of a boy will be subjected to varying pressure, thus producing lines with many variations of width.

There are, of course, other ways of imitating marble, but this method is perhaps the most foolproof under school-shop conditions, especially with young boys. When the streaking is dry, the penholder should be assembled, the bushing inserted, and, if desired, the bottom should be covered with felt or a piece of blotter.

BIRDHOUSES

An attractive and novel wren house, made almost entirely of scraps of roofing paper, is shown in Figure 32. The colored sand or crushed rock with which this roofing paper is coated adds much to its appearance.

Figure 32 clearly shows the construction of the wren house. The $\frac{7}{8}$-in. diameter entrance hole can be made with dividers. This can be done by placing the dividers on the reverse side of the paper and turning it several times. The round plug thus formed can be pushed out with the fingers after several turns without cutting clear through to the sandstone coating on the other side of the roofing paper. The conical roof is held in shape with three pieces of wire pushed through the paper and clinched.

The bottom should be fastened with flathead nails which should not be driven in all the way. This will facilitate withdrawing the nails for removal of the bottom for cleaning.

Provision always should be made for ventilation of roofing-paper birdhouses in order to avoid overheating. In addition, they should be located where they will be in the shade for most of the day.

Figure 33 gives the details of another type of wren house. Rough box lumber is just as good as planed lumber, and perhaps even better, for birdhouses of this kind.

Figure 34 shows several designs of this type of birdhouse. The size and shape of the house, and the location and size of the opening can all be varied to attract different kinds of birds.

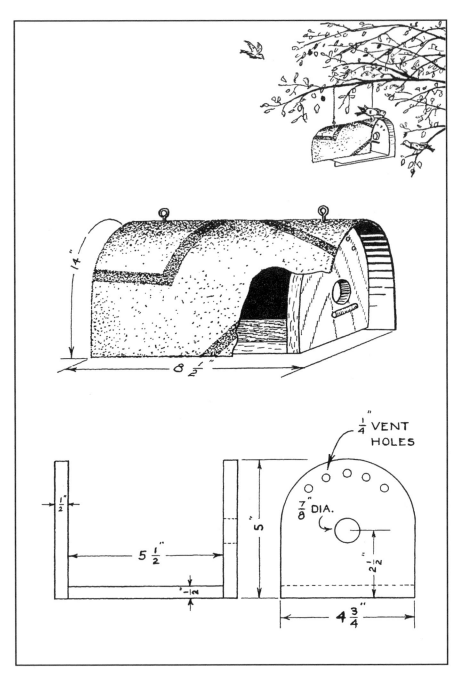

Fig. 33. A wren house.

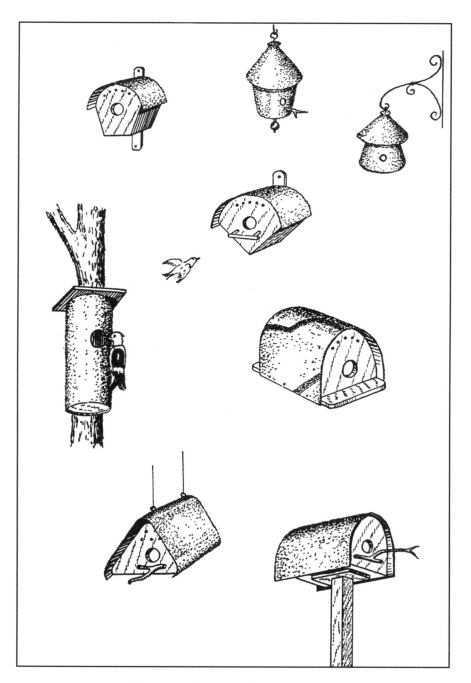

Fig. 34. Birdhouse suggestions.

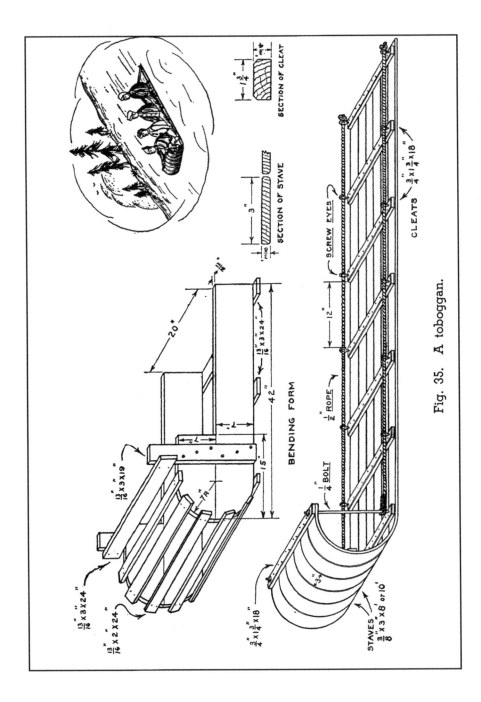

SECTION OF CLEAT

SECTION OF STAVE

BENDING FORM

Fig. 35. A toboggan.

TOBOGGAN

In order to be able to make a toboggan, a bending form, as shown in Figure 35, must be made first. Such a form should become a permanent device in a school shop.

Toboggan staves should be made of oak or hickory. Oak, however, is more readily obtainable, and is easily worked and bent. Care should be taken to select wood with straight grain for the staves. All edges of the staves should be rounded to a radius of about ⅛ in. to prevent splintering and slivering at the corners. The cleats, nine in number,

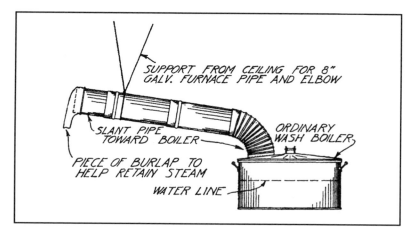

Fig. 36. A steam box.

for 8-ft. staves, may be made of oak. All top edges should be chamfered and the screw holes should be bored and countersunk.

At least 30 inches of the staves must be steamed or soaked at one time and preparatory to bending. Steaming is much more preferable to soaking and generally more practical, for it is difficult to find a container large enough to accommodate 30 in. of the staves.

A suitable steam box can be easily built of wood to the required length. A hole should be cut in the bottom of the steam box and then it should be set over a kettle or pan of water on a gas plate. The staves now should be placed in the box keeping them separated so as to permit the steam to penetrate all surfaces. The open end of the box should be closed with wet burlap to prevent the escape of the steam. The staves

[47]

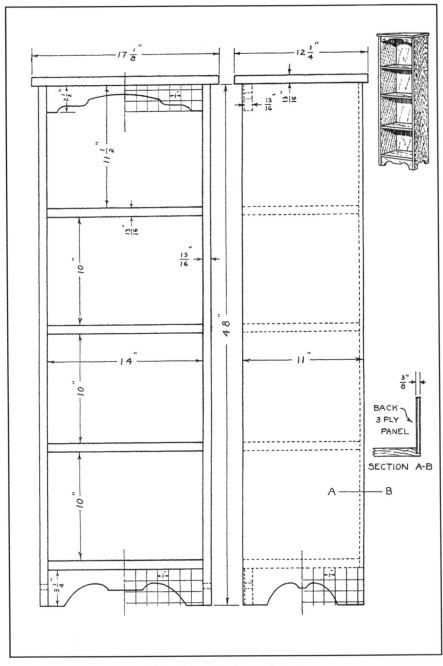

Fig. 37. A pier cabinet.

should be steamed for four or five hours. Another method of making a steam box is shown in Figure 36.

When the staves are sufficiently steamed, the bending form shown in Figure 35 should be fastened on its side so that it will not move when the staves are being bent. One end of a stave then should be placed under the edge of the 3-in. cleat on the bending form and be bent around. The other end of the stave should be clamped or tied to the other end of the form. The staves should be removed from the steam box one at a time and be placed in the bending form. The staves should dry on the form at least twenty-four hours.

A toboggan cleat should be fastened to the front end of the staves first. Next, the cleat at the bottom of the curve should be fastened in place, and then the one midway between these two. After these three front cleats have been fastened in position, the one near the end of the toboggan should be placed. The remaining cleats then should be spaced evenly and fastened in place. The staves must not be butted edge to edge; a scant ⅛ in. should be allowed between them for possible swelling. A long bolt is used to keep the front end bent, but a piece of chain or leather may be used in its stead. If a bolt is used, the head should be countersunk. Chain or leather braces may be held with screws. This bracing is necessary because, in starting the toboggan, it is sometimes pulled by the curved part and, unless it is braced, damage or breakage may result.

The screw eyes which hold the rope handles should be quite heavy. If suitable screw eyes are not obtainable, ½-in. pipe straps will serve in their stead.

The toboggan requires at least two coats of linseed oil, or a mixture of half turpentine and half oil, which will penetrate well.

PIER CABINET

The pier cabinet, shown in Figure 37, is simple in construction, and the dimensions may be easily varied to meet any special requirements. The number of shelves, their spacing, and the width and depth of the cabinet can be changed without much trouble. However, if the height is increased, it is well to make the cabinet deeper to prevent any tendency to tip forward.

Pine, poplar, basswood, or redwood are suited for the construction. The shelves should preferably be housed in stop dadoes. Through dadoes for the shelves, however, greatly simplify the construction and should be used for lack of ability to make good stop dadoes.

Unless such joints fit well, they add little or nothing to the strength and detract much from the appearance. In some instances nailed butt joints are used in construction of this kind. If the shelves are perfectly squared and the lumber is flat, a good job can be produced with the use of butt joints. Section A-B, Figure 37, shows how to fit the back into a rabbet cut into the ends of the cabinet. The back and the ornamental top and bottom rails add greatly to the rigidity of the structure.

Fig. 38. An upholstered footstool.

UPHOLSTERED FOOTSTOOL

Nicely figured wood should be used, if possible, for the ends of the footstool shown in Figure 38. The rest of the stool is covered with upholstering.

Attention is called to the nailing blocks which are fastened to the inside surfaces of the ends. These blocks may be fastened first and then the side rails may be nailed to them or preferably fastened with screws. Another method of assembly is to fasten the side rails to the nailing blocks before the nailing blocks are fastened to the ends. The three pieces which make up the top then may be nailed in place.

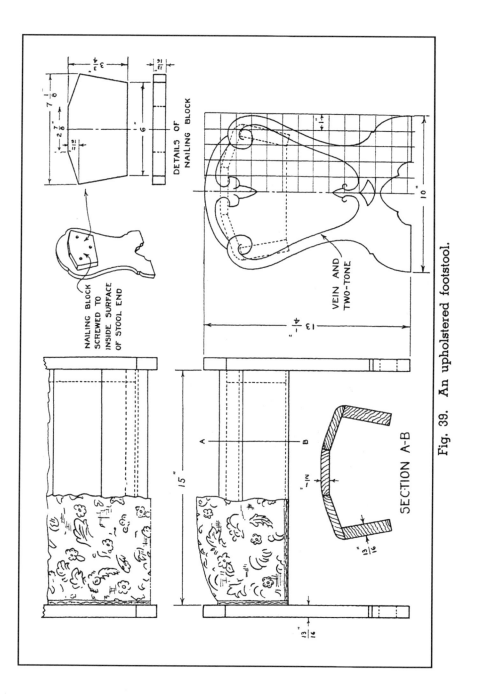

Fig. 39. An upholstered footstool.

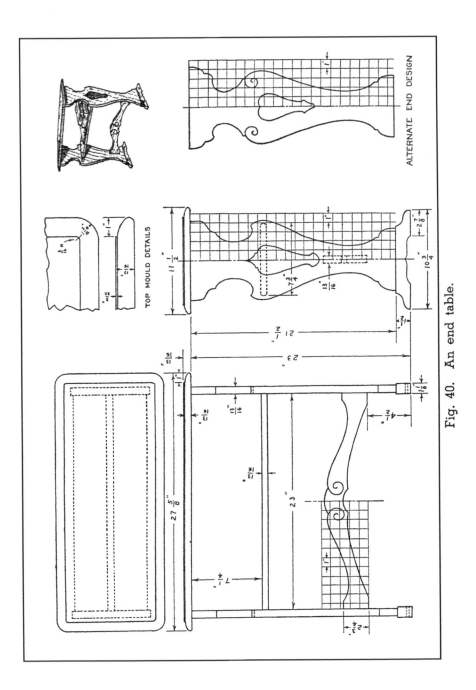

Fig. 40. An end table.

When finishing the footstool, the center section of the ends should be made lighter in tone than the rest of the project. This two-toning can be accomplished either by staining only the outside portions and leaving the inside natural, or by staining the outside portions with water stain and, when this is dry, staining the entire ends with either another coat of water stain or with oil stain. Too great a contrast should be avoided.

The surface enrichment can be simplified by using only scrolls on the ends or by using a leaf design similar to that shown in Figure 18. Figure 12 shows the type of gouge used for the veining.

END TABLE

There always seems to be room and use for one more end table. It may be for this reason that end tables are such popular projects in school and home workshops.

The end table shown in Figure 40 is well within the ability of the junior-high-school boy. Walnut, mahogany, or gumwood is well suited for this table, but cheaper woods such as poplar, basswood, or butternut may be used.

A trough may be used in place of the shelf shown in Figure 40. Whether a shelf or a trough is used, great care must be taken in locating it otherwise the table may not stand flat on the floor.

The design on the ends of the table may be a separate piece or veined in with a 1/16- or ⅛-in. straight carving gouge, as shown in Figure 12.

The best joint for stretcher and shelf is mortise-and-tenon, but dowel joints may be used. Butt joints, held with flathead screws neatly concealed with putty or with wood plugs, also may be used.

The top mold can be easily made with a rabbet plane and a smooth plane if a shaper is not available. A molding under the top such as is used in the stool shown in Figure 53 also could be used on this table.

The designs on the ends of the table may be finished either lighter or darker than the rest of the table. To make them darker, they should first be stained with water stain, avoiding the gouge lines. When this is dry, the entire project, including the design and the gouge lines, should be stained either with oil or water stain. If desired, the molding around the top may be stained to correspond with the design in the ends. If the designs are to be lighter than the rest of the table, they should be shellacked or oiled before staining the table.

An alternate design for the end of this table also is shown in Figure 40. Scrolls could be used to enrich this alternate end as indicated. A full-sized pattern for laying out the scrolls is shown at B, Figure 18.

END TABLE

The end table in Figure 41 will appeal to the more talented or skillful pupil and home craftsman.

The construction details are shown in Figure 42. Walnut, mahogany, or gumwood may be used. The carving is not difficult and it can all be done with two or three gouges. The contour of the carving may be obtained from the illustration in Figure 41. No machinery is necessary to make this table but, of course, the use of a jig or band saw would make the work much easier. The best way to connect the stretchers and the ends is with the mortise-and-tenon joint and here again, if a circular saw is available, tenons can be quickly and accurately made.

The mold on the table top is made with a rabbet plane and a smooth plane if a shaper is not available. The molding under the top is hand made. The grooves running across this molding are cut with a 1/16- or ⅛-in. straight carving gouge like the one shown in Figure 12. The details of this molding and the method of fastening it to the underside of the top are shown in Figure 42.

This table should be stained, filled, shellacked, and varnished. It might also be stained, shellacked, and waxed. If a varnish finish is to be applied, it should be given a very thin coat of shellac after staining, so that the filler will wipe off the surface well without leaving a cloudy effect due to a smudge of filler which might adhere to the surface of the wood. The shellac must be very thin otherwise it will partially fill the pores and reduce their holding power for the filler.

Fig. 41. An end table.

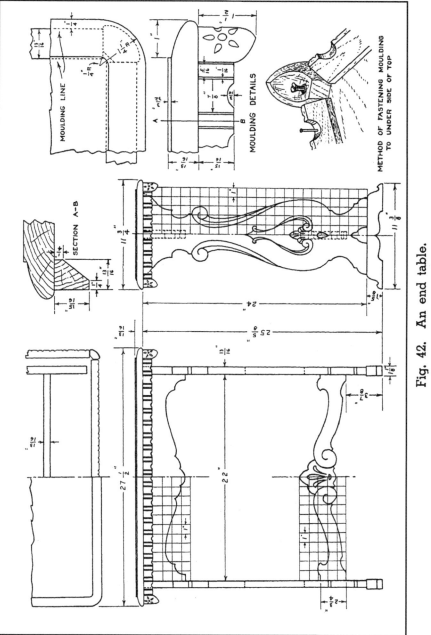

Fig. 42. An end table.

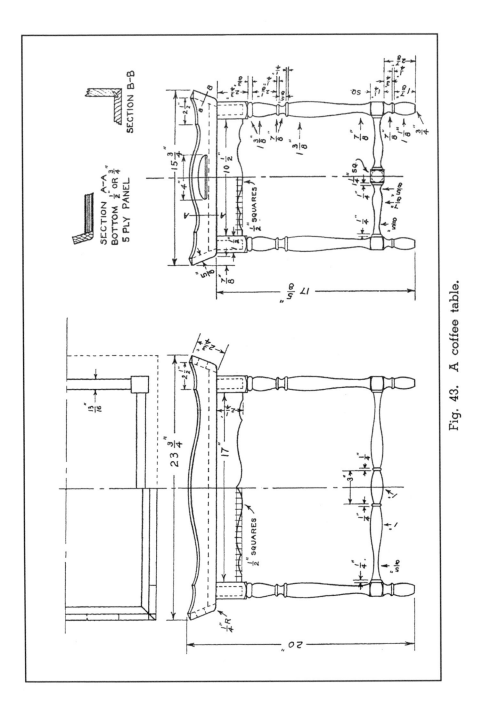

Fig. 43. A coffee table.

COFFEE TABLE

The coffee table has become a popular piece of furniture in our homes. The table shown in Figure 43 has a permanent top or tray, that is, the tray is fastened to the table. The tray, of course, could be made removable.

Walnut, mahogany, birch, or gumwood are suitable for this table. There are no special problems involved in its construction but careful, accurate workmanship is necessary, especially in the construction of the tray. The tray corners should be reinforced with a spline as shown in Section B-B, Figure 43. Glue blocks should be used at the corners of the tray so that each corner may be properly drawn up with individual clamps. Either mortise-and-tenon or dowel joints will serve equally well for joining the rails and legs.

Stain, shellac, and either wax or varnish make a good finish. If a varnish finish is to be used on an open-grained wood, it will be necessary to use filler before varnishing. The filler should be applied after the stain has dried. A very thin coat of shellac may be applied before filling so that the filler will wipe off the surface without leaving a cloudy surface. However, if the shellac is applied too heavily the open grain will be partially filled with shellac and then the filler will not stick in the pores.

If desired, a piece of clear or opaque glass may be used on the bottom of the tray. If glass is used a molding will be required around the inside edge of the tray to hold the glass in place and to finish the edge.

The substitution of a flat top in place of the tray would convert this project into a bench. All of the dimensions are about right for this alternative project.

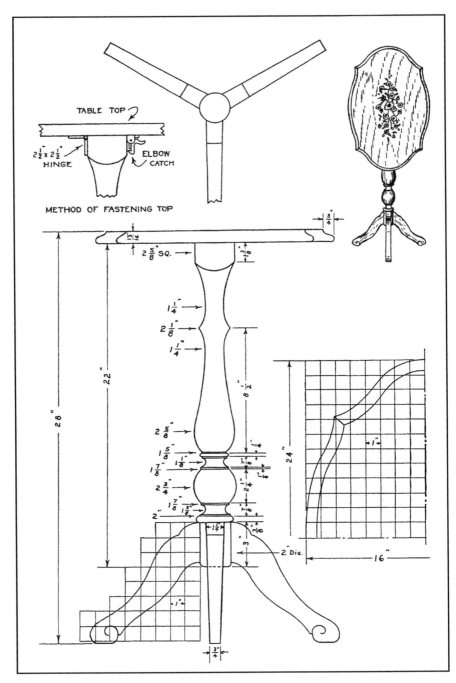

TABLE TOP

$2\frac{1}{2}" \times 2\frac{1}{2}"$
HINGE

ELBOW CATCH

METHOD OF FASTENING TOP

Fig. 44. A tilt-top table.

TILT-TOP TABLE

The tilt-top table is always ready for use and may be set aside into a corner to act as a decorative piece of furniture.

Figure 44 gives the details of an attractive serviceable table of this sort. If the table is to have a stained finish, use walnut, mahogany, birch, or gumwood. If an opaque finish such as enamel is used it may be made of cheaper woods such as poplar or pine.

In this project the pedestal is usually the first part to be made. The material to make the required thickness for the pedestal should be glued, and while this is drying the three legs may be laid out and cut. At the point where the legs contact the pedestal it will be necessary to fit them to the curved section. To do this, a cylinder slightly smaller in diameter than the bottom of the pedestal should be turned and a sheet of sandpaper glued around it. While this sanding drum is revolving in the lathe, the legs should be held against the sandpaper until they are cut to make good contact with the base of the pedestal. The holes for the dowels should be bored in the legs before shaping the joint. The scrolls on the legs are optional and may be veined in with a gouge of the type shown in Figure 12.

The edge of the top may be molded as desired. The top tilts on a hinge and is held in a horizontal position with an ordinary elbow catch.

Inlay, hand-painted decorations, or decalcomanias are often used to decorate the tops of tilt-top tables.

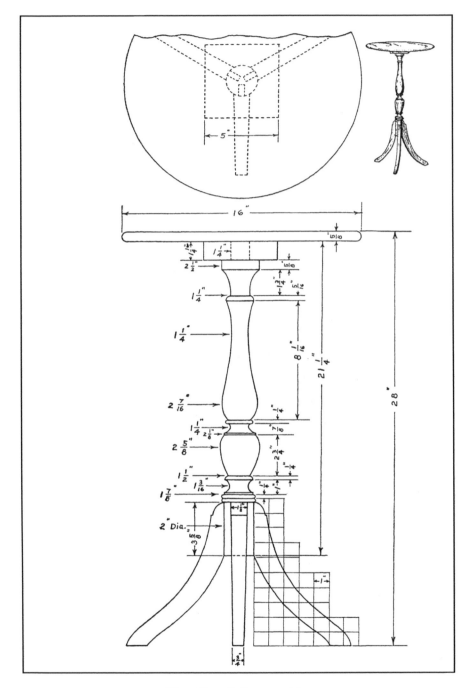

Fig. 45.   A lamp table.

LAMP TABLE

It has come to be quite generally accepted that several chairs in the living room require their own lamp. The lamp table in Figure 45 may be used with almost any armchair or davenport.

If the table is to be given a stained finish use walnut, mahogany, birch, or gumwood. If the table will be finished with enamel, cheaper woods may be used, such as poplar or pine.

When making the pedestal for this table, the tenon on the top end must be turned. This tenon fits into a hole bored in the 5-in. square block on which the top rests. The three legs must be fitted to the curve of the lower end of the pedestal. To fit the legs to the pedestal, a cylinder of scrap wood, slightly smaller in diameter than the lower end of the pedestal, must be turned and a sheet of sandpaper must be glued around it. The legs should be held against this sandpaper-covered cylinder as it revolves in the lathe until they are cut so as to make good contact with the base of the pedestal. The holes for the dowels in the legs should be made before shaping the joint on the legs with the sandpaper cylinder.

The table should be finished with stain, shellac, and either wax or varnish. For a varnish finish on open-grained wood, a filler will be necessary. After staining, a very thin coat of shellac may be applied so that the filler will wipe from the surface without leaving a cloudy effect. If the shellac is too thick, the grain will be partially filled, and its holding power for filler will be destroyed.

This table could be readily converted into a tilt-top table by using a larger top and making use of the tilting arrangement shown in Figure 44.

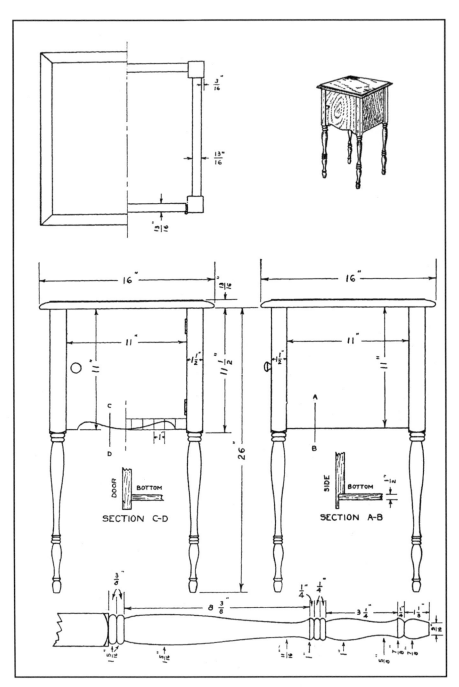

Fig. 46. A bedside table.

BEDSIDE TABLE

The bedside table in Figure 46 may also be used as a smoking cabinet, or a chair-side table to hold a lamp, or for many of the numerous purposes to which small tables are put in our homes.

Walnut, mahogany, birch, or poplar are well suited for its construction, which is quite simple. Those not having a lathe on which to turn the legs could substitute square legs similar to those shown in Figure 47. Doweled butt joints may be used in the construction, but the side and back rails could be rabbeted to fit into grooves cut into the legs. If desired, the side and back rails could be decorated by a curve similar to that used at the bottom of the door. In Section A-B, Figure 46, is shown the manner of fitting the bottom into a rabbet cut into the side and back rails. With this construction, the bottom can be easily fitted after the cabinet is assembled and it can then be nailed in place and strengthened with a few glue blocks if desired.

The door may be either solid or plywood. The thumb mold used on the top can be made with rabbet plane and a smooth plane if a shaper is not available. Of course, a plain, square-edged top could be used or some other form of mold could be substituted for that shown.

A sewing cabinet. See page 70.

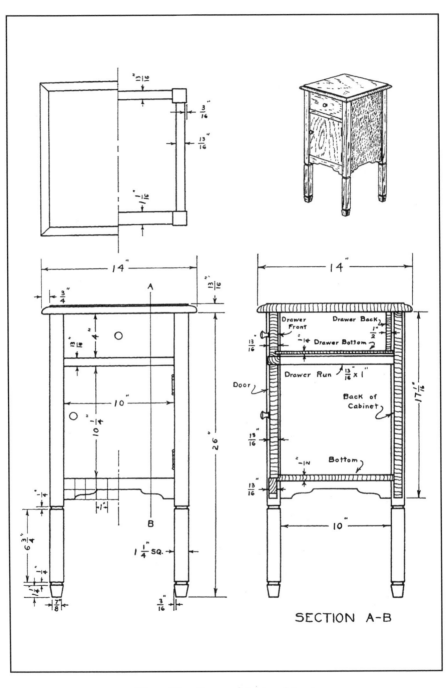

Fig. 47. A smoking cabinet.

SMOKING CABINET

The smoking cabinet shown in Figure 47 may also be used as a sewing cabinet or as a bedside table.

Poplar, pine, or basswood may be used in the construction of this simple project. No machinery whatever is required. All joints with the exception of the drawer construction may be doweled butt joints. The most simple form of drawer construction may be used such as a simple rabbeted drawer front and a groove in the front and sides of the drawer for the bottom to fit into. The door may be one piece as shown, or it may be made of plywood.

The cut-out portion in the legs may be done with a gouge and a round file. These cut-out sections should then be carefully sanded with sandpaper wound tightly around a piece of dowel stick. If a lathe is available, a turned leg may be made.

The table-top mold can be easily made with a rabbet plane and a smooth plane if a shaper is not available. A chamfered-edge top or a plain square-edged top also may be used. The bottom can be fitted after the cabinet is assembled, and it can be supported on cleats or be held with glue blocks.

A wall shelf. See page 20.

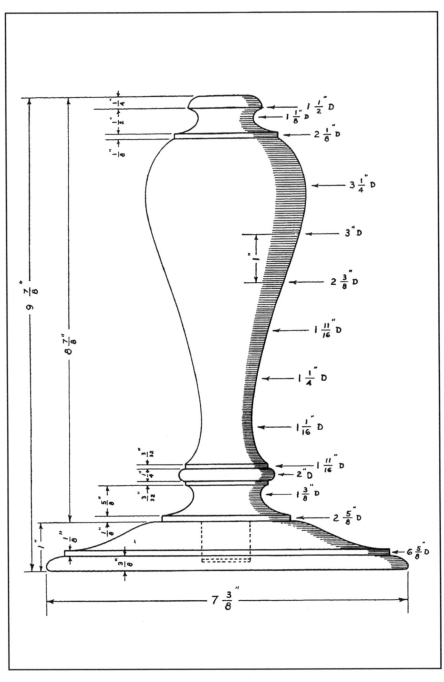

Fig. 48. A turned table lamp.

TABLE LAMP

In the construction of a lamp, such as shown in Figure 48, it is usually better to glue up material for the standard to the required thickness instead of turning the standard from one piece. One-piece construction involving thick material is often subject to checking. Checking is avoided by gluing up the thickness. When cutting the material for the standard, a sufficient amount should be allowed for the tenon which fits into the base of the lamp.

The hole through the center for the wire may be made before or after turning. If the hole is made before turning, it should be plugged at each end so that the work can be centered in the lathe. The tenon should be finished before turning the hole in the base. When the tenon is finished first, it can be fitted more easily by trial than if an attempt is made to turn it and the hole to measure.

If the lamp is to be given a stained finish, the two parts should not be glued together until after shellacking. It is very convenient to sand such work while it is revolving in the lathe. Even if an enameled finish is to be used, the priming coat of shellac can be sanded with the work between the lathe centers.

Lamps made in school should be wired in the shop under the supervision of the instructor, otherwise the boy may not do the work properly and a fire hazard may result. The wiring of a lamp is a valuable lesson in home mechanics and one which may be used many times.

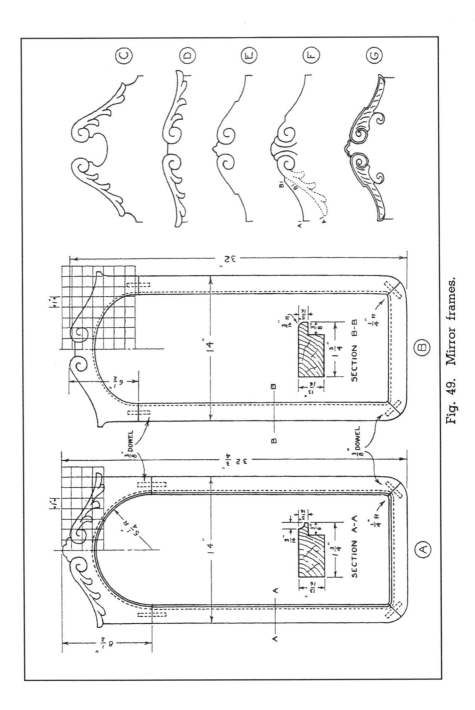

Fig. 49. Mirror frames.

MIRROR FRAMES

Either of the mirrors, shown in Figure 49, may be used with a console table.

These mirror frames may be made of walnut, mahogany, or gumwood. Careful, accurate workmanship is required in the cutting and fitting of the joints. A trial assembly, with all dowels in place, but without the use of glue, should be made to be sure that the joints are all tight.

A full-sized detail of the leaf design used at the top of A, Figure 49, is shown at B, Figure 18. This leaf design may be veined and then stained slightly darker for contrast, or it may be carved and applied to the frame. The design could also be carved in low relief directly on the frame.

B, Figure 49, is identical with A with the exception of the top design. The ornament on this frame is merely a scroll which has been laid out with a part of the pattern which is shown full size at B, Figure 18.

C, D, E, F, and G, Figure 49, show a few of the possibilities in the use of the pattern in B, Figure 18, for producing different designs. Any of the designs shown at the right of Figure 49 can be used on a mirror frame. Different effects can be produced with these patterns or parts of the patterns. Additions to the pattern details also may be made as shown in G, Figure 49. The use of such patterns will stimulate an appreciation of design and develop originality. For school use such patterns should be made of metal. Figure 19 shows how they can be cut with a coping saw having a metal-cutting blade.

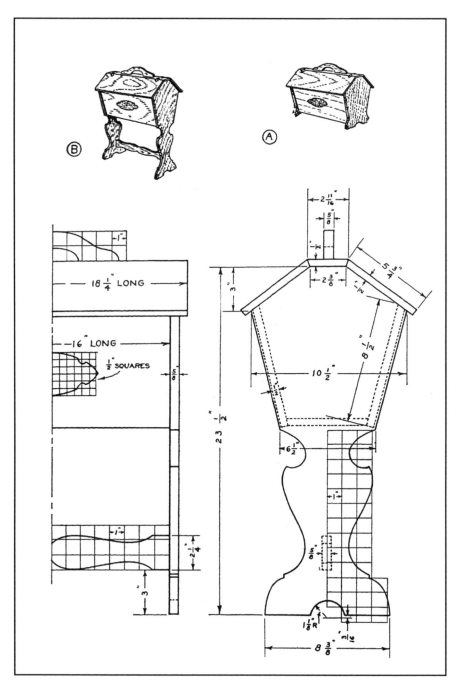

Fig. 50. A sewing cabinet.

SEWING CABINET

A feature of the sewing cabinet in Figure 50, which will appeal to many, is its simplicity of construction, for which no machinery or special tools are required.

Pine, poplar, or basswood are ideal woods to use for this project. The joints may be nailed butt joints with the brads neatly set and the holes carefully filled with putty. The handle, however, should be fastened to the upper cross member by two 1¼-in. screws. The screws should be driven through the cross member and into the handle so that they will not be visible. The designs on the sides of the cabinet may be either veined or applied. They may be stained either darker or lighter than the rest of the cabinet. Figure 12 shows the type of gouge used for veining.

It is best to cut the covers about ½ in. wider than the finished width and then, when the beveled edge at the top along the hinged joint fits well, cut the covers to the finished width.

This type of sewing cabinet sometimes is enameled, but the more conservative finish is stain, shellac, and either wax or varnish. Surface hinges are quite appropriate for this cabinet and they can be applied very easily by anyone. The proper application of butt hinges, on the other hand, requires careful workmanship and skill.

A, Figure 50, is a table model of the same cabinet. The dimensions are identical with those of the floor model, except that the ends are shortened and feet are added to them in order to secure stability and improve the appearance. The table model would be improved if it were made of ⅜-in. material.

A sliding tray for scissors, spools, needles, and other small articles can be added to either of these cabinets. Two small cleats should be fastened inside of the cabinet for the tray to rest on. The tray should be about one half the width of the cabinet so that when it is pushed to either side one may reach down into the cabinet without removing it.

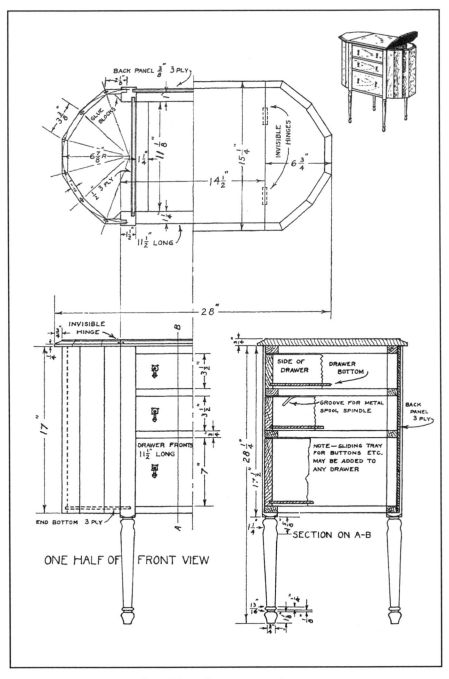

Fig. 51. A sewing cabinet.

MARTHA WASHINGTON SEWING CABINET

The Martha Washington sewing cabinet, unlike a number of other time-honored furniture designs which have been perpetuated largely for the sentiment connected with their history, is a decidedly practical and beautiful piece of furniture. The cabinet contains plenty of room in which to keep all of the sewing equipment as well as the odds and ends of material which accumulate and which the thrifty woman likes to keep in her sewing nook.

The construction of this sewing cabinet is a work of precision and should not be attempted until an accurate full-sized working drawing is made. The sizes and angles of the staves which make up the end pockets should be taken directly from the full-sized drawing. Accuracy in determining and in cutting the angles on the end-pocket staves cannot be overemphasized, for the least deviation from the correct angle will cause the whole construction to vary in size and shape. Glue blocks should be used to aid in clamping the end staves together, and a trial assembly should be made to insure a perfect fit before gluing. When cutting the groove in the staves for the spline, a jig is required, for if the sharp edge of the staves is run against the ripping fence it may catch or run under the fence and spoil the piece. Even though the sharp corner did not catch between the ripping fence and saw table, it would be very difficult to hold the piece at the correct angle throughout the cut. The jig may be made out of any cull stock and it is a good problem to test out the ingenuity and resourcefulness of the student.

The drawer frames may be joined with dowels or with a short tenon and a corresponding groove cut in each end of the rails. If the drawer frames are doweled to the legs the construction will be practical and strong. The sliding tray suggested in the drawing may be divided into compartments to suit the particular requirements of the user. The top molding is easily made with a circular saw and a rabbet plane, or entirely with a rabbet plane, and although this molding may be omitted, it adds much to the appearance of the interestingly shaped top.

Mahogany, walnut, birch, or gumwood are suitable woods to use for this cabinet and a dull or else rubbed varnish finish is recommended; but when lack of time or proper facilities do not permit the application of such a finish, a shellac waxed finish or a lacquer finish may be applied. Occasionally these cabinets are painted or enameled but the preference is for a transparent finish.

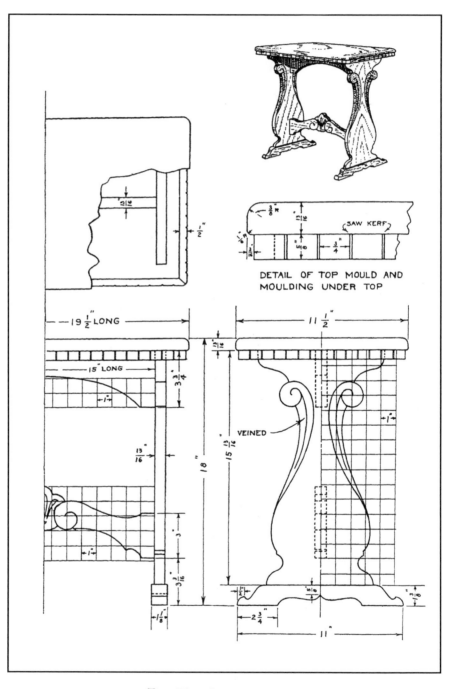

DETAIL OF TOP MOULD AND
MOULDING UNDER TOP

SAW KERF

19 ½″ LONG

15″ LONG

11 ½″

VEINED

Fig. 52. A radio bench.

RADIO BENCH

To construct the radio bench, walnut, mahogany, or gumwood should be used. Basswood or poplar may be used by those who find difficulty in working the harder woods. The beauty of this bench lies in the flowing curves of the end designs, the lower stretcher, and the fine-arched upper stretcher or rail all of which give it a sturdy appearance.

The best joints for the stretcher and the upper rail are mortise-and-tenon; however, dowel joints will be quite satisfactory. Butt joints held with flathead screws neatly concealed with putty or wood plugs also may be used. The feet may be doweled to the ends or may be fastened with screws.

For the best effect, the scrolls or leaves on the ends should be stained slightly darker than the rest of the bench. The leaves should first be water stained, but the outside gouge lines should be avoided with this staining. The inside gouge lines, however, such as the termination of the scroll and the gouge line extending down the center of the leaf should be stained. When dry, the entire project including all the gouge lines should be stained with either oil or water stain. The bench then should be finished in the usual manner with shellac, wax, or varnish using a filler if necessary for the varnish finish.

With a few minor changes in the top this bench can be readily changed into a coffee table.

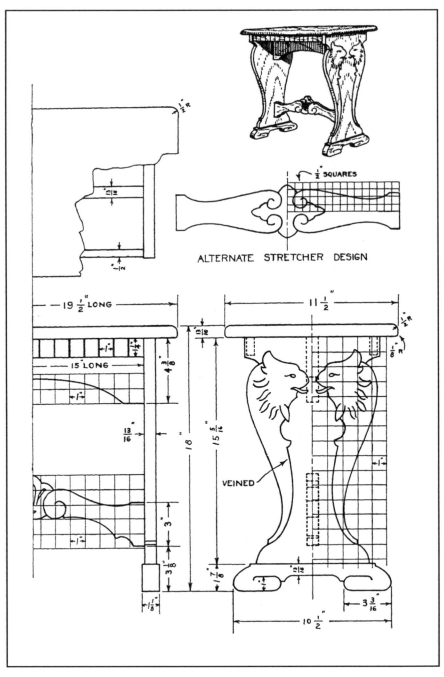

½" SQUARES

ALTERNATE STRETCHER DESIGN

VEINED

Fig. 53. A radio bench.

RADIO BENCH

The radio bench shown in Figure 53 is much like the one shown in Figure 52 except for the end design.

Walnut, mahogany, or gumwood may be used, although poplar and basswood are very good. Chestnut, oak, or ash, however, are not suited for this kind of work.

The best joints for the stretcher are, of course, mortise-and-tenon, but dowel joints may be used. Butt joints, held with flathead screws and neatly concealed with putty or wood plugs also are suitable. The feet may be doweled to the ends of this bench or else be fastened with screws. The lion's-head motifs used on the ends can be easily adapted from the design in Figure 54 on page 78. If this pattern is to be used a great deal it is well to make it of metal as shown in Figure 19. If desired, two simple scrolls may be used in place of the lion's head.

The lion's-head design will stand out better if it is stained slightly darker than the rest of the project, and it should be water stained first. The outside gouge lines must not be stained at this time. All inside gouge lines, however, such as the eyes and the lines representing the lion's mane should be stained. When dry, the entire project, including that part just stained as well as all gouge lines, should be stained with oil or water stain. The bench should be finished as usual with shellac, wax, or varnish using a filler if necessary for the varnish finish. If the alternative stretcher design is used the center section of the stretcher should be stained darker to correspond with the staining of the lion's head.

If desired, this bench may be upholstered.

Fig. 54. A lion's-head design (full size).

ENLARGING DRAWINGS WITH AN OPAQUE PROJECTION LANTERN

Exact enlargements of any drawing in this book, or any book or magazine, may be made by simply projecting the drawing with an opaque projection lantern and then drawing the outline as shown in Figure 55.

Fig. 55.   Enlarging a drawing with
an opaque projection lantern.

Projection lanterns of the type shown in Figure 55 can be purchased in toy shops and in department stores for a very nominal price.

Some schools have an opaque projection lantern for use in the academic department for the projection of maps, pictures, and the like. The industrial-arts instructor will find such a lantern well adapted for enlarging drawings. Some of the lanterns used in schools permit the insertion of an entire book into the lantern. The book can be maneuvered so that the illustration or drawing to be enlarged will be projected.

To enlarge a drawing with the cheaper lantern, like the one shown in Figure 55, it is best to cut that part of the page containing the drawing and insert it in the lantern or trace the outline on tracing paper and insert the tracing in the lantern. While these lanterns are designed to project post-card-size pictures, clippings to be projected need not be of post-card dimensions. Smaller clippings may be held by first inserting in the slot a piece of mica and then inserting the clipping behind the mica, which can be bought in most hardware stores. Washed photographic film or clear celluloid should not be used for this purpose, as the heat from the electric-light bulbs may ignite either.

The lantern shown in Figure 55 reverses the picture or drawing, that is, the right is projected to the left and the left to the right. This, of course, is immaterial because most designs used in the shop are bi-symmetrical. Those designs having detail which must not be reversed may be projected onto tracing paper and then reversed to their original position by turning the tracing paper over.